The Project Management

Project Scheduling – Simplified!

Michael B Bender, MBA, PMP, CSM

The Project Management Mini-Series

Project Scheduling - Simplified!
1st Edition, February, 2016

© 2016 Michael B Bender. All rights reserved.
Published by: Ally Publishing Group, Sugar Grove, IL 60554

Please forward comments and suggestions to:
  AllyPublishingGroup@AllyBusiness.com

ISBN-10: 1-940441-12-9
ISBN-13: 978-1-940441-12-2

DEDICATION

To my sister Heidi. Your optimism and relentless pursuit of common sense provide motivation and clarity; however, your ever-present love is my greatest inspiration.

PREFACE

ABOUT THE SERIES

I specifically designed the Project Management Mini-Series for busy project managers. Project management is a vast topic. While no particular aspect is difficult, mastering all necessary skills to make a project successful takes time.

You'll face many issues in your journey to master the discipline; some you'll handle nicely, but some may involve skills new to you. You'll want quick, professional-level answers to specific project management questions. I designed the Project Management Mini-Series for just such occasions.

The books are short, inexpensive, written for professional project managers, and designed to be easy-to-read. They get to the point, demonstrate how to apply skills, offer tools and techniques, and then allow you to get on your way.

The series is not just for new project managers. I offer three levels of books, color-coded for quick recognition:

- Simplified! (Hunter Green) for new or novice project managers
- Skilled (Royal Blue) for novice to moderate skill levels
- Advanced (Gold) for more advanced techniques

Some key features I included:

- Templates, forms, charts and checklists, with descriptions on how to use them.
- Electronic copies of the templates and forms, which you can download from my company's web site: www.AllyBusiness.com/PMTools/. Adjust them for your own style and needs.
- "Tricks of the Trade," which offers specific techniques I and many colleagues have used to accomplish goals and tasks.

I hope you find the series useful. Please feel free to e-mail me with comments and suggestions. I set up a special e-mail address for this series: PM-Mini-Series@AllyBusiness.com.

ABOUT THE BOOK

Project scheduling is one of the most basic, yet most important, tools for any project manager. Fortunately, it's generally one of the easiest to master. The math is rudimentary (don't worry, if you graduated 5th grade you'll be fine). The process is straightforward and easily executed. Even better news: the results are powerful.

Projects, by their nature, include a collection of interdependent activities that must be coordinated for successful project execution. The results of project scheduling include a precedence diagram that clearly depicts these interdependencies. When we factor in duration estimates for these activities, the project schedule presents itself in beautiful clarity.

In this book, we introduce you to the concept of *critical path*. This "path" identifies all activities that are schedule-critical. Other tasks may not be as tightly tied to schedule, meaning if they're late by a small amount, your project is still on track. Understanding this key concept allows project managers to improve resource allocations, handle problems more easily, and even help out other project managers.

I hope you enjoy the book, and…

May all your projects be successful!

ACKNOWLEDGEMENTS

I want to thank my good friend, Ms. Kimi Hirotsu Ziemski, for all her help and support, and for serving as the inspiration for this book.

Also special thanks to Mr. Brian J. Croft and Ms. Vicki White for their excellent jobs in editing.

CONTENTS

1 INTRODUCTION TO PROJECT SCHEDULING

Project scheduling is the act of properly sequencing project activities and establishing the times activities should start and finish. For example, before I go grocery shopping, I first have to create a list, get my wallet, and drive to the store; this might take me 20 minutes. Then, I enter the store, go down aisles, select my groceries, and pay for them; after that, I can take them home and put them away.

While this all seems simple enough, how many times have you gone grocery shopping and forgotten your list or money? Do you use recyclable shopping bags? If so, you need to both put them in the car and remember to take them into the store. And how many times have you arrived home after shopping, only to discover you forgot to get something?

While these small setbacks might generate some frustration, similar problems in projects can be catastrophic. Our goal for project scheduling is more than just determining when activities should be executed—it's also to help ensure we do these activities right, and in a timely manner.

What We Need to Start

Project scheduling, like all activities, has its own tasks that must be completed before we start. There are really only three. First, we need the complete list of activities. We get this from the *Work Breakdown Structure* (WBS) (see: *Project Work – Simplified!*, Bender, 2013). Second, we need duration estimates for each activity. Finally, we need to know what's needed to start each activity.

The Work Breakdown Structure identifies all activities in the project. The WBS does not identify any activity sequencing, resources, schedules, or anything else related to our quest here; it simply identifies all activities we need to accomplish.

There are two kinds of activity estimates: *effort* and *duration*. Effort estimates identify the actual, dedicated time all individuals will spend on the activity. Duration estimates identify how long the activity will take on the calendar.

Finally, we need to know *inputs* into each activity. Inputs are any item, artifact, or document needed to do the job. The inputs tell us what activities have to be finished before we start the next activity. Using our grocery shopping example, creating the list and getting my wallet are inputs to "Drive to the store".

What We Create (Our Deliverable)

The result of project scheduling is generally a *precedence diagram* depicting task sequences. These diagrams usually include start and end dates for activities—in essence, our schedule. Most precedence diagrams also depict the project's critical path. This path identifies the series of project activities that is time-critical. Many advanced project managers forget that not all project activities are time-critical. In fact, many projects can experience a task schedule slip without experiencing *any* impact on the project at all. Understanding which activities are time-critical and which aren't, allows project managers to better allocate resources, handle problems, and interface with other ongoing organizational work.

Our Scope

Project scheduling, for the purposes of this book, involves sequencing and identifying start and end dates for activities within the project. We include a detailed discussion of critical path. We also present basic concepts of estimating. Finally, we examine practical applications of the project schedule, precedence diagram and critical path.

2 ESTIMATING BASICS

Our goal for this chapter is not to present a thorough treatment of estimating; however, a basic understanding is required. Those familiar with estimating basics can feel free to skip this chapter.

Accuracy of Estimates

I frequently stand in front of classes and ask a simple question: "What is an estimate?" The answer most often given is that an estimate is a guess. I take it one step further: an estimate is a prediction of the future. The estimator predicts the sequence of events, along with anticipated interruptions and distractions to determine the estimate. Certainly, there exists some inaccuracy. The level of accuracy depends on several factors, including the level of task definition, degree of risk, number of people assigned, level of complexity, and others. Therefore, it is customary to express an estimate as a range rather than a single number.

Early estimates tend to be less accurate as the level of project definition is lessor. As we progress through the project, we understand it better and estimates tend to be more accurate. It's not unusual for early estimates to have a range of ± 30% or more. These are called ROM (*Rough Order of Magnitude*) estimates. With a well-developed WBS, however, tasks might typically have a range of ± 10% or even ± 7%. These are called *definitive* or *engineering* estimates. For these estimates, we rarely include the range as this level is sufficient for accurate project scheduling.

Effort-Driven Activities vs. Duration-Driven Activities

Most activities are effort-driven, meaning that the duration depends on the amount of effort individuals apply to the task. Brick-laying and data entry are effort-driven activities. Other activities are duration-driven, meaning that they don't depend on individuals, but simply on time. Curing concrete is a duration-driven activity. It doesn't require any resources, the concrete simply needs enough time to cure. Preparing a turkey for dinner is effort-driven, while roasting the turkey is duration-driven.

Effort vs. Duration Estimates

There are two kinds of estimates for effort-driven activities: *effort estimates* and *duration estimates*. Effort estimates predict the actual amount of labor involved in completing an activity. We usually measure this labor in *Full-Time Equivalents,* or FTEs (we used to call these "man hours," but that designation has been deemed politically incorrect). FTEs are the amount of time a single person would spend performing a given activity. This excludes interruptions, breaks, and other issues that prevent work on the task. *Duration* is the amount of time the activity takes on a calendar.

Let's consider a simple activity involving data entry. We have a large stack of completed paper forms and one individual responsible for entering this information into a computer. If we assume that 1) the FTE estimate for this activity is 40 hours, 2) this is the only activity for which this individual is responsible, and 3) that there are no external interruptions, we might ask: can this individual complete this activity in one week?

Sadly, the answer is no. This individual will take coffee and lunch breaks, and may have to complete administrative forms such as timesheets or attend meetings. Therefore, this activity will, in total, might take six (6) days.

Effect of Team Size

Now, let's add another individual with equal aptitude and dedication to this activity. Initially, you might assume that the activity will now only take 3 days as it's spread across two people. However, these two people would have to coordinate their work and may exhibit some conflict. Therefore, the task may actually take 3 and a half days.

This example assumes the task can be performed efficiently by a single individual and it can be easily subdivided for two people. In general, each activity has an ideal team size. Refinishing a basement, for example, tends to be performed more efficiently by 3 or 4 people. New studies indicate that writing software modules is best performed by teams of 2 people.

Savvy project managers work with their subject matter experts (SMEs) to determine the optimum team size for each activity, they try to get the right resources.

Ownership and Estimates

Many project managers make the mistake of estimating tasks themselves. They sit in their cube or office, lay out the project, and come up with estimates without outside assistance. Extensive research suggests the best estimates are provided by those doing the work. There are two key reasons for this. First, the individual (supposedly) is a subject matter expert (SME), and, therefore, is more familiar with the work than someone else. If the individual is not a SME, the project manager should work with the individual to help account for the learning curve.

The second reason is perhaps more important. By providing the estimate, the individual takes ownership of the task. This generates commitment, motivation, and pride. This is one of the key methods to help build a strong project culture within your team. Simply put:

Ownership Builds Commitment!

Effect of Task Size in Estimating

In general, the smaller the task, the more accurate the estimate. This is another reason why early estimates tend to be less accurate. Early estimates address the overall project or large sections of the project. Once the project manager and team have created a detailed WBS, the team can accurately estimate each task and generate a more accurate schedule.

Occasionally, a team member may have difficulty estimating a task. One technique I use for this is to have the individual break the task down into smaller steps. Have them create a check-list of all the items they need to do. Once created, they will usually be able to estimate the task more easily and more accurately.

Over- or Under-Estimating

Most people pad estimates. They do this for several reasons. First, they need to account for interruptions, problems, risks, and other "unknowns". Second, they want to look good to their boss. Third, padding the estimate makes their life easier by reducing the time pressure. The problem with this is that padded estimates extends the project duration unnecessarily. Other people tend to underestimate. They feel everything will go well without considering risks or other issues.

In general, I encourage people to resist padding or underestimating. I call them *50-50* estimates. By this I mean the individual has a 50% chance of completing early and 50% chance of finishing late. Since projects contain many tasks, the early tasks cancel out the late tasks and I make my schedule while reducing my project duration.

Some activities require more reliability. If you are preparing for a demonstration for a client, go ahead and add contingency time to address problems that may occur.

3 ACTIVITY SEQUENCING

Activity sequencing is a simple process of determining which activities must be done first and which need to follow. For example, you can't erect the wall of a new house unless you've completed the foundation. You also can't add the roof until you've finished the walls. Other tasks can be done in parallel. For example, once wall frames are in, electricians, plumbers, and HVAC (heating, ventilation, and air conditioning) teams can work in parallel (assuming they can stay out of each other's way). The more activities we can do in parallel, the faster we can build our house. Our challenge, as project managers, is to parallelize as much as possible, to shorten the overall project schedule without having teams get in each other's way.

First, some definitions. The *predecessor* is the task that comes before another task, and *successors* are tasks that follow. Predecessors give us what we need to do our job; they provide us with inputs. If our activity is erecting wall frames, our predecessors might include:

- Complete foundation
- Acquire frame wood and nails
- Complete blueprints (to know where to place walls, windows, and doors)
- Acquire framing tools

Now that all the predecessors are complete, we can start framing.

After we've built the walls, then electricians, plumbers, and HVAC teams will come in and run electrical wiring, plumbing, and heating/AC ducts. These are our successors. A simple precedence diagram (see Figure 1) captures these activities.

Figure 1: Framing Wall Precedence Diagram

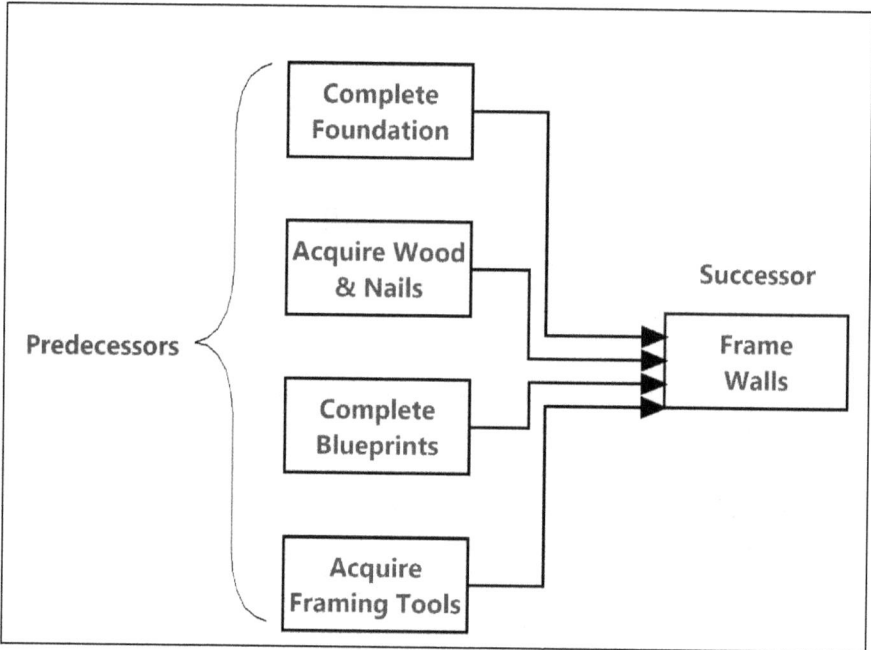

The Lexicon

Before we proceed further, it's appropriate to introduce the formal lexicon for activity sequencing.

We call any diagram depicting the sequence of activities in a project a *Network Diagram*. The diagram above is a special type of network diagram called a *precedence diagram*. It is also known as *Activity on Node* (or AON), as the boxes (or nodes) represent activities in the project. Another form of network diagram is an *Activity on Arrow* (AOA) diagram, where the arrows represent activities and the nodes (usually shown as circles) represent states of completion. Such diagrams are also known as *Arrow Diagrams*. Figure 2 shows the AOA form of our earlier precedence diagram.

Figure 2: Frame Walls Arrow Diagram

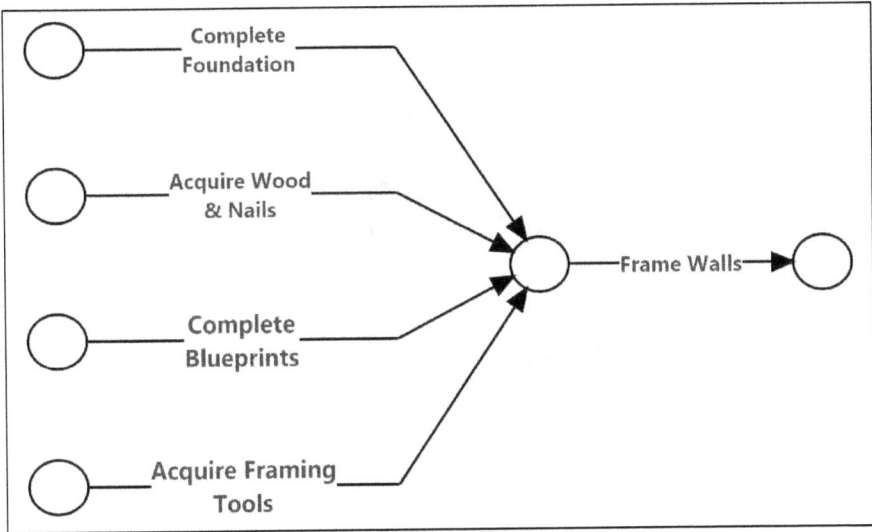

The arrow diagram was once more common in large projects—that is, until the advent of computers. Precedence diagrams are easier to program, and have therefore become more prevalent. The advantage of the arrow diagram is that you can time-scale the arrows; however, few (if any) software packages offer this option so, for this text, we'll limit our discussion to precedence diagrams.

Types of Inter-Task Relationships

The term *dependency* refers to the linkage between two tasks. The successor *depends on* the predecessor since the predecessor must complete before the successor starts. In the above example, erecting wall frames depends on completing the foundation, acquiring the wood and nails, completing the blueprints, and acquiring the framing tools. This represents one type of inter-task relationship, where predecessors must finish before a successor task starts. There are, in fact, four types of inter-task relationships. These are: *finish-to-start, start-to-start, finish-to-finish,* and *start-to-finish* as described below.

Finish-to-Start (FS). In the above example, all dependencies are *finish-to-start,* meaning we must finish all these activities before we can start wood framing. This is the most common form of dependency in most projects.

Figure 3: Finish-to-Start Relationship

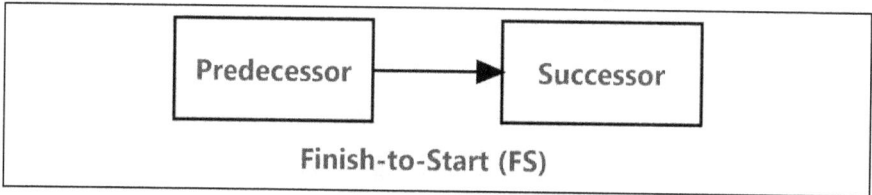

```
┌─────────────────────────────────────────────────┐
│   ┌──────────────┐          ┌──────────────┐     │
│   │ Predecessor  ├────────▶ │  Successor   │     │
│   └──────────────┘          └──────────────┘     │
│              Finish-to-Start (FS)                 │
└─────────────────────────────────────────────────┘
```

Start-to-Start (SS). With this dependence, task B cannot start until task A starts. This is a forced dependency. In the above example, plumbers and electricians do not exhibit a start-to-start dependency, because neither needs to wait for the other to start; they *can* start at the same time, but they don't *have* to.

A typical example of a start-to-start relationship would be a supervisor monitoring work of a subordinate. In the above example, if the supervisor monitored the work of electricians, the supervisor's job would have to start at the same time electricians begin work. The precedence diagram form of the SS relationship is shown below.

Figure 4: Start-to-Start (SS) Relationship

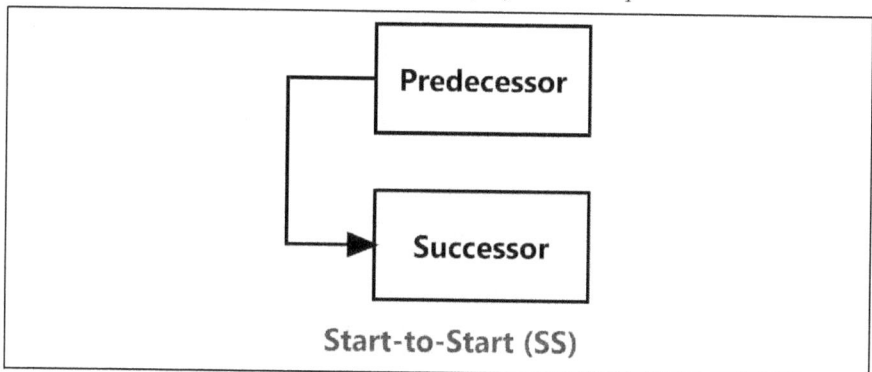

```
┌─────────────────────────────────────────────────┐
│              ┌──────────────────────┐            │
│       ┌──────┤    Predecessor       │            │
│       │      └──────────────────────┘            │
│       │      ┌──────────────────────┐            │
│       └────▶ │     Successor        │            │
│              └──────────────────────┘            │
│              Start-to-Start (SS)                  │
└─────────────────────────────────────────────────┘
```

Finish-to-Finish (FF). The finish-to-finish relationship is similar to the start-to-start, except the successor cannot finish until the predecessor finishes. A typical example of this would include proofreading a manuscript—the proofreader cannot finish her work until the author finishes his.

These types of relationships are frequently contractual. For example, a customer of a new computer system may require the project team to hold their hand while they get trained on the new system; the task "handholding" cannot finish until training finishes.

Figure 5: Finish-to-Finish Relationship

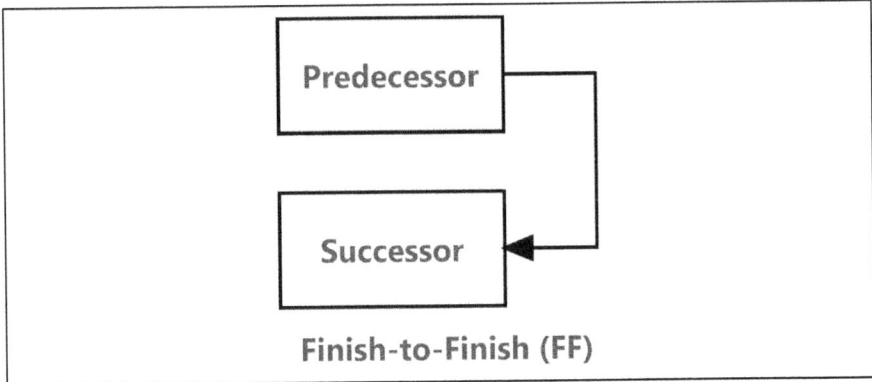

Predecessor

Successor

Finish-to-Finish (FF)

Start-to-Finish (SF). This is the least common of the relationships. In this scenario, the predecessor cannot finish until the successor starts. A typical example is a guard at a guard gate. The first-shift guard is the predecessor, and the second-shift guard is the successor. The first-shift guard cannot leave the gate unguarded, so he cannot finish his task until the second-shift guard arrives and starts work.

Figure 6: Start-to-Finish Relationship

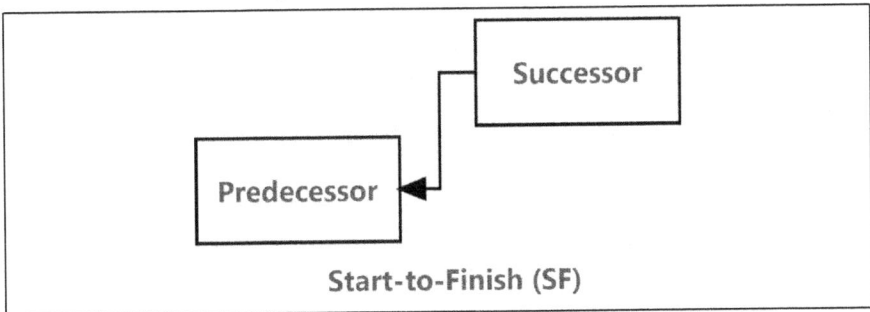

Successor

Predecessor

Start-to-Finish (SF)

Hammocks. Hammocks involve a special and common combination of SS and FF relationships. An example of a hammock occurs when you outsource work. The vendor represents one task (let's call it task A), and the team member responsible for monitoring the vendor's work represents task B. The task "monitor" must start when the vendor starts (a SS relationship), and will finish when the vendor finishes (a FF relationship).

Note: There is another definition of hammocks in the project management arena. For our series (and for my projects), I use the definition above.

Figure 7: Hammock Relationship

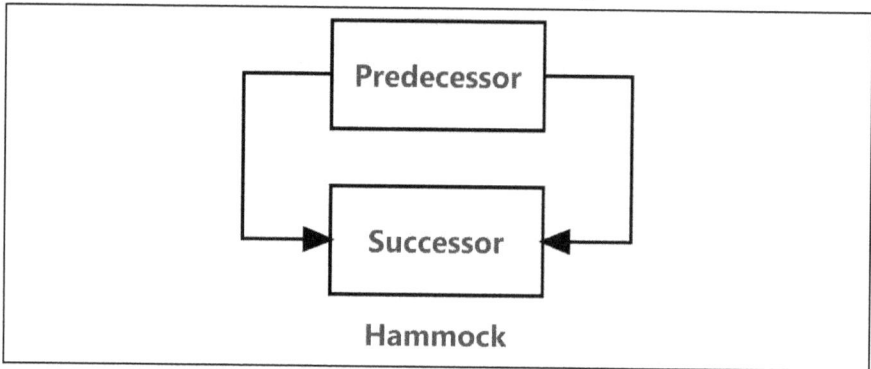

Types of Dependencies

Modern project management identifies three different types of dependencies. The most common is called *mandatory*. Mandatory dependencies are based on the mechanics of the work itself, as demonstrated in our earlier examples. You physically can't erect walls unless the foundation is complete and you have blueprints, tools, and wood. Similarly, a proofreader will need a draft copy of a document before he can begin proofreading.

The second type of dependency is called discretionary. *Discretionary* dependencies are not based on the mechanics of the work, but on other external or environmental conditions, such as best practices and resource limitations. For example, let's assume the HVAC team tends to get in the way of electricians and plumbers which may slow our overall progress. We might use discretionary dependencies to hold off plumbers and electricians until HVAC work is complete, thus making the project more efficient. You can also use discretionary dependencies to handle resource limitations.

The final type of dependency is *external*. External dependencies identify tasks outside the project that must be completed before tasks inside can begin. For example, let's assume the home we're building is only one house in a development. Let's further assume that while we're building our house, a contractor is paving the road. At some point, we'll have to delay work as they pave the road as our team won't be able to get into the development. We use an external dependency indicated by a dashed line for this purpose.

Proper Precedence Diagramming Techniques

Proper diagramming techniques are critical to successful management. While the examples in this book are simple, imagine what a diagram might look like with a few hundred tasks. It's important to establish good habits early… you'll appreciate the time spent when you start running larger projects.

Here are some tips to create clean, easy-to-read precedence diagrams:

- Start and end your precedence diagrams with a milestone node—or "start" and "end" node—as I do in the diagrams above. Milestone nodes are usually depicted as a diamond or oval.

- Every dependency should have its own connection. That way, you can instantly know the number of predecessors and successors for each task..

- If you must cross connections, either "jump over" or "go under" another dependency line, otherwise you don't know if they connect or don't connect.

- Always enter a task from the left and exit from the right. Never use the top or bottom of the task node.

Examples of good and poor diagramming techniques are shown below.

Figure 8: Poor Diagramming Technique

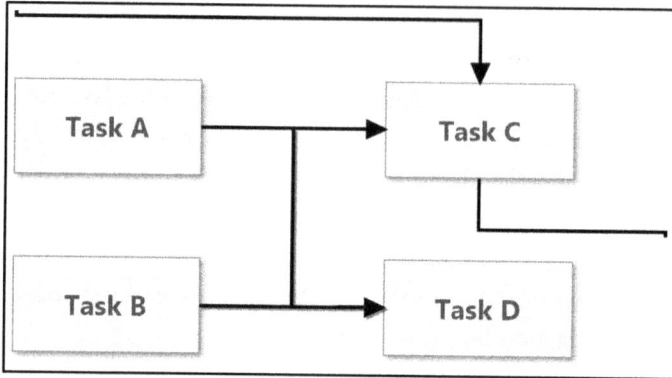

Figure 9: Good Diagramming Technique

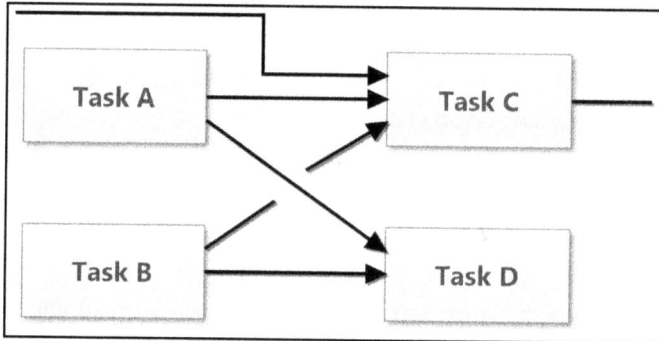

4 CRITICAL PATH

In my opinion, critical path is one of the strongest tools in the project manager's tool chest. Before we explore its power, let's examine what it is.

When most people first hear the term *critical path,* they usually assume it represents the most important, "mission-critical" tasks in a project. However, the term defines tasks that are "schedule critical", not mission critical. The *critical path* is the path of activities with the longest duration. It defines the fastest time in which you can complete the project. Furthermore, if any task along these paths is delayed for any reason, the overall project is delayed. Not all tasks exhibit this characteristic. Let's look at a simple example.

Consider a project with three tasks: A, B, and C. Task B depends on A (in a FS relationship), but task C can run parallel to both A and B, as shown in Figure 10. The duration of each task is represented; let's assume these numbers represent days.

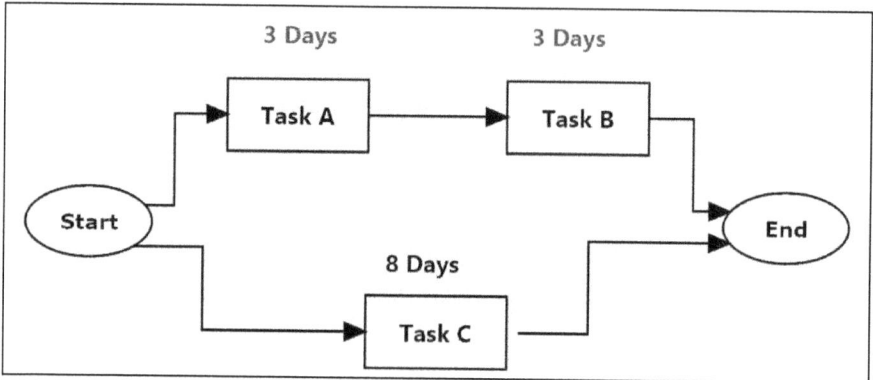

Figure 10: Simple Critical Path

Note that task C will take eight days, while the combination of A and B will only take six days. In this example, task C represents the critical path, because if it is delayed or takes longer than estimated, the entire project will be delayed. However, if the combination of tasks A and B is delayed by less than two days, the project can still complete in eight days. *Float* is the term used to represent the time a task can "float" on a calendar without impacting the project end date. In this example, tasks A and B have two days of float; in other words, these individuals have eight days to complete six days of work.

Critical Path for Small Projects

Establishing the critical path for small projects (say, under 12 tasks) frequently can be accomplished through inspection. Remember the critical path is the path with the longest duration through the network. How many paths do you see in Figure 11?

Figure 11: Critical Path by Inspection

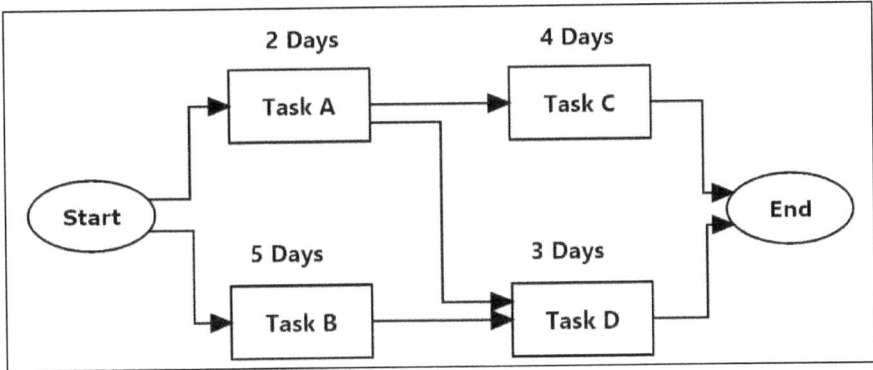

If you answered *three,* you're correct. Here are the paths:

A – C

A – D

B – D

To determine the critical path, add the durations of each path and find the longest one. Here are the calculations:

A – C   duration: 6 days

A – D   duration: 5 days

B – D   duration: 8 days

The longest path is B – D, which makes it the critical path.

While this method is fast, it generally doesn't allow you to compute the float of each task and becomes confusing with complex networks.

Critical Path for Medium & Large Projects

Certainly, most projects have more than four tasks, and we frequently want to compute the float for each task. Let's look at how we compute the critical path for a more complex project. This will also give us the float of each task. For our example, we'll assume all relationships are FS, and that duration estimates for all activities are known and relatively accurate.

Computing critical path involves two passes through the network. The first pass, called the *forward pass,* determines the earliest times a task can start and finish. It also establishes the fastest time in which we can complete the project. Once the forward pass is completed, we can conduct the *backward pass*. The backward pass computes the latest times a task can start and finish without delaying the project.

Note that in Figure 12, we don't include units for durations. They may represent days, weeks, quarters, minutes, or any other unit of duration. However, they can't represent months as the duration of months is inconsistent. Also note that critical path works regardless of units (as long as they're of a consistent length).

Figure 12: Critical Path – Initial Precedence Diagram

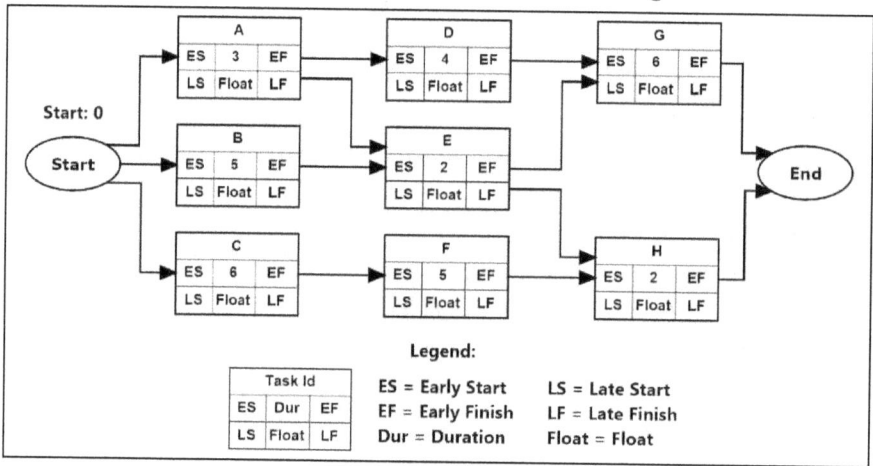

Forward Pass. The forward pass starts at the beginning of the project and, as its name implies, moves forward through the project. We start the first task(s) at time zero (0), because no time has passed. The earliest finish time is simply the start time plus the duration:

$$Finish = Start + Duration$$

Early start and early finish, by definition, are the earliest points in time a task can start or finish. To compute these figures, start from the left side of the diagram (project start) and continually ask yourself, "What is the earliest time I can start and finish a task?" We then proceed to the right through the project network.

The exact steps for computing the forward pass for Figure 13 are shown below.

1. Start the project on the beginning of day 0.
   The earliest time the first tasks (A, B, and C) can start is day 0. Add the duration of that task to the early start to determine the earliest time the task can finish. Task A takes three days; therefore, the earliest time it can finish is the beginning of day 3. Task B can end on day 5, and task C van end on day 6.

2. The earliest day task D can start is day 3. Note that task E has to wait for both A and B to complete. The earliest time we can start task E is on day 5.

3. Proceed from left to right until you get to the end of the project. This project will take 15 days.

Once complete, the diagram shows the earliest times tasks can start and finish. It also shows the shortest time to complete the project—in this case, 15 days.

Figure 13: Critical Path – Forward Pass

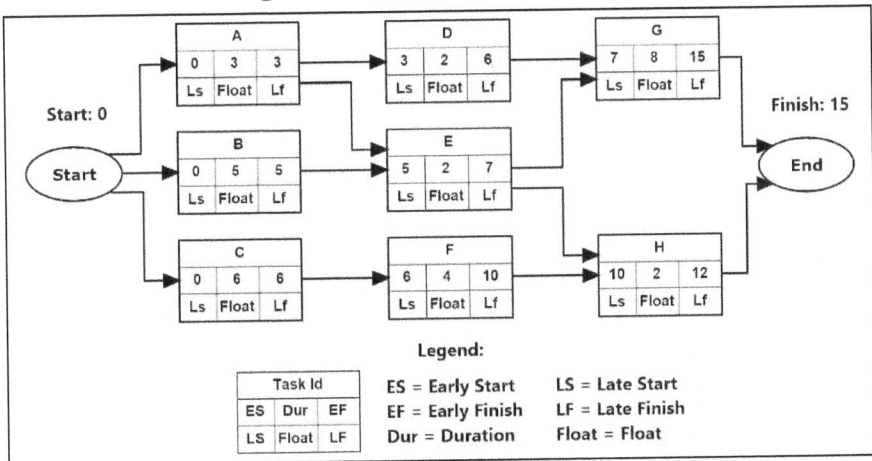

Backward Pass. As its name implies, with the backward pass, we do everything backwards. We determine late start and late finish in a manner exactly the opposite of computing early start and early finish. Instead of proceeding from left to right, we move from right to left. And, instead of asking, "What is the *earliest* time we can *start* a task?"

we ask, "What is the *latest* time we can *finish* a task without delaying the project or any successors?"

For this process, we simply rewrite the equation:

Start = Finish – Duration

Here are the steps for computing the backward pass for Figure 14.

1. Start at the end of the project. Task G must end by day 15. Therefore, it must start by day 7. Similarly, Task H must end on day 15; therefore it must start on day 13.

2. Take either path backwards. Task D must finish by day 7 to prevent delaying task G. Therefore, it must start by day 5. Task F cannot delay H, so it must finish by day 13; therefore, it must start by day 9.

3. Note task E. It cannot delay either tasks G or H. Since task G must start by day 7, and task H can wait until day 13, task E must finish by day 7 to prevent delaying G. Therefore, it must start by day 5.

4. Continue working right to left until you reach the start of the project.

The completed backward pass is captured in Figure 14.

Figure 14: Critical Path – Backward Pass

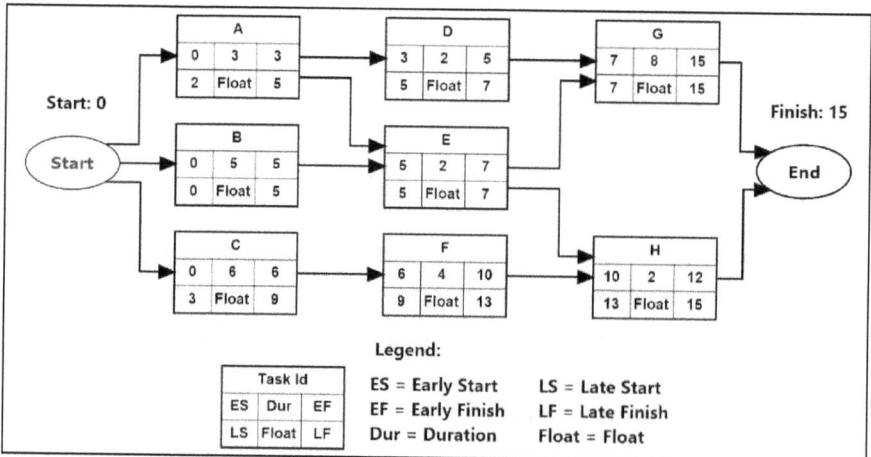

We now have everything we need to compute the critical path. We have the earliest times we can start and finish tasks, as well as the latest times we can start and finish tasks without delaying our project.

We mentioned earlier that float is the amount of time a task can "float" on a calendar without delaying our project. The equation for float is simply:

Float = Late Finish – Early Finish[1]

To compute float for each task, simply subtract the early finish from the late finish, as shown in Figure 15.

Figure 15: Completed Critical Path Diagram

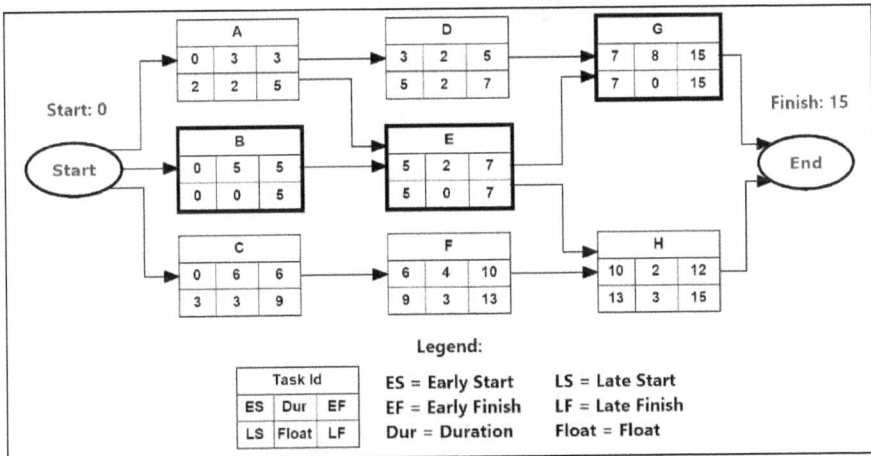

Can you see the critical path? It's the path of activities with zero floats. If any task along this path is delayed, for any reason, it would extend the entire project. Now consider task A which has two days of float. This means task A can be delayed by two days without affecting project duration. Similarly, task F can be delayed by three days.

---

[1] In this example, you can use late and early starts as well; however, this becomes problematic in more advanced scheduling activities. Establish good habits by using finish times.

5 PRACTICAL APPLICATIONS

Now that we know how to compute critical path, we can explore its importance as a project scheduling tool.

Resource Allocation

The first question concerning resources becomes, "Where do I put my best people?" The answer should be obvious: you put your best people on the critical path. Now, let's define "best people." Many project managers assume this means the most competent people. This is not necessarily useful. I prefer to put my most *responsible* people on the critical path—that is, those most committed to getting the job done right. If they feel they don't have sufficient subject matter expertise, they'll get the needed resources. If there's a problem with the task, they'll let me know so I can help them resolve it. These are the people I trust to make sure the task is done on time. They won't let interruptions interfere with their schedule, they focus on making sure the activity meets requirements and is properly inspected, and that all associated activities are completed on time.

I don't put new people on the critical path until they prove themselves. This also goes for vendors; if at all possible, I only put my most responsible vendors on the critical path.

Trainees go on tasks with the most float. This gives me time to work with them if problems arise.

Handling Problems

Scenario 1: Delays off the Critical Path. This is usually the simplest problem to handle. If the delay is less than the float, there's no schedule problem. You simply help the individual through the problem and monitor the situation closely.

Scenario 2: Delays on the Critical Path. While challenging, you'll find this less of a burden with a solid critical path network diagram. I simply find individuals on tasks with float and move them to the troubled activity. While they may not be the ideal people, they can certainly provide assistance and help move things along.

Scenario 3: Unexpected Emergencies. Your boss walks into your office and says there's a problem with another client. He needs two people to go to Oshkosh, Wisconsin for four days. Who do you send? A quick look at your critical path offers your answer. You choose people assigned to activities with at least 4 days of float. Of course, as above, these might not be the most reliable people on your team. You can back them up by providing phone support from more reliable and experienced people. While this may result in a small delay, it's substantially better than taking a complete four-day hit.

Problems that Change the Critical Path

Sometimes problems aren't simple. Consider task D in the Figure 15. It has a float of 2 days. If it exhibits a problem that causes a delay that exceeds 2 days, it now creates a new critical path.

In this situation, the project manager must consider moving resources. This, of course, can be disruptive to the overall project, so I proceed with caution when this happens. Frequently, I'll simply have a more experienced person help the troubled activity and take the schedule hit rather than move everyone. Sometimes, however, reallocating resources is required.

Summary

As you can see, critical path can be a very powerful tool. Personally, I'm not sure how someone can successfully run a project without it as it helps resource allocation and problem solving better than any other tool I know.

6 TRICKS OF THE TRADE

Assume an Ideal Team

Every project—as well as every task within a project—has an ideal team. This is the ideal number and skill sets of individuals that will accomplish the project (or task) the fastest.

When I build my first precedence diagram, I use only mandatory dependencies. I then add in external dependencies and a minimum of best-practice discretionary dependencies. This, in essence, defines the ideal team needed for the project, as well as the fastest time to complete the project. It tells me what skill sets are needed and when they're needed. I use this tool to ask for the ideal team from management. While I may not get this team, I at least know what to ask for. As I acquire my actual team, I'll adjust the precedence diagram accordingly using discretionary dependencies. This, de facto, extends the duration of the project. I then use this fact to help me negotiate for a better team.

Schedule as Early as Possible

There are several theories regarding when to schedule tasks with float. Some contend they should be scheduled as late as possible. This keeps time pressure on the task performer to complete on time.

29

Others contend tasks with float should be scheduled as early as possible to reduce risk. If problems arise, the task performer has some time to fix the problem without impacting the project schedule. However, if the task owner knows there is float, they can tend to procrastinate.

The way you handle this may depend on your style and your team. Personally, I prefer to schedule as early as possible to reduce risk. I then use my leadership skills to prevent procrastination. This may not work if you have a difficult team. One solution is to use the critical path as a motivational tool as described in the next section.

Critical Path as a Motivational Tool

This is one of my favorite methods for motivating a team. Classically, I'll have one or two senior team members and a lot of novice or less-experienced team members. I put my most experienced and responsible people on the critical path at the start of the project. I then celebrate their wins when they complete on time and indicate that's how you move up in my teams. I only put my most trusted people on the critical path. If members want to get there, they must demonstrate they can perform the task by its early finish date. As less-experienced people demonstrate they can complete tasks by their early finish date, I reward them by moving them onto the critical path.

This technique offers two benefits. First, it helps me reduce schedule risk and allows me to move my best people onto tasks with float. That way, when problems do arise, I can move my best people onto the problem without impacting the schedule.

The second benefit is likely more important. As I tend to put my best people on the critical path, so do other project managers. This means the best people are always on the critical path and under tight time pressures, which can burn them out. By putting them on tasks with float, I can both give them a break and have them available to tackle problems.

Using Critical Path to Build the Team Culture

This technique also helps build the team culture. Using the critical path as a reward mechanism encourages team members to complete tasks on time and with high quality. I've found many delays occur because individuals rush through tasks, frequently ignoring requirements or not quality-checking their work. As this causes schedule delays, these folks don't receive the reward of being placed on the critical path. They eventually learn tasks aren't complete until all requirements have been met and are quality reviewed; they start to form better habits and start completing tasks on time. Then—and only then—do I feel comfortable placing them on the critical path.

This creates a culture of highly-responsible team members. It's amazing how well and how quickly these teams will complete projects!

7 SUMMARY

In this short book we've addressed the basic techniques for estimating activities, scheduling activities, and developing a solid project culture within the team.

Estimating involves predicting how long an activity will take. There are effort-driven activities where the estimate is based on the amount of labor hours required to complete the work, and duration-driven activities which are independent of labor. For effort-driven activities, the estimator must consider the interruptions, distractions, and other delays inherent in an organization to determine the actual duration for the task.

Once we have the estimates, we can create a precedence diagram to determine the sequence of work. This diagram effectively shows the flow of work throughout the project. Once complete, we can determine the range of dates each activity can take using critical path methodology. This method establishes the time-critical activities in a project, helps us allocate resources across the project, handle emergencies, and perhaps most importantly, build a strong project culture within the team.

Personally, I find critical path to be one of my strongest tools for planning and managing a project. Spend the time to do it right. You'll be glad you did.

Good luck, and may all your projects be successful!

ABOUT THE AUTHOR

Mr. Bender, president of Ally Strategic Partners, Ltd., is an accomplished international speaker, author and seminar leader in the business management field. Mr. Bender holds an electrical engineering degree from Rutgers University and an MBA specializing in project management. Mr. Bender also holds Project Management Professional (PMP) and Certified Scrum Master (CSM) certifications.

Specializing in all areas of strategic planning, work flow management and resource management, Mr. Bender is a frequent speaker for DeVry University – Becker Professional Education, the American Management Association and many other companies, organizations and universities. Mr. Bender's keynote speeches focus on advanced concepts in resource management across strategic plans, programs and portfolios for industry, non-profit, educational and government sectors.

Mr. Bender began his career in high-technology fields. Specializing in computer systems development, Mr. Bender worked both as a subject matter expert and project manager on such projects as the Hubbell Space Telescope, the U.S. weather radar system, air traffic control systems in three continents, satellite launches, cable television automation systems, and many other technology-based projects. Through this experience, Mr. Bender developed his unique skills in advanced program management, resource allocation and strategic planning.

Mr. Benders published works are included in the bibliography that follows. For more information, please visit Ally's web site at www.AllyBusiness.com.

BIBLIOGRAPHY

Bender, M. (2010). *A manager's guide to project management.* Upper Saddle River, NJ: Pearson as FT Press.

Bender, M. (2013). *Definingp project work - simplified!* Sugar Grove, IL: Ally Publishing Group.

Bender, M. (2013). *Project risk management - simplified!* Sugar Grove, IL: Ally Publishing Group.

Bender, M. (2016). *The high-performance organization: the effects of oculture on organizational performance.* Sugar Grove, IL: Ally Publishing Group.

Hamilton, B., & Bender, M. (2015). The intersection of senior sanagement optimism and projectr risk management. *Proceedings of the Intellectbase International Consortium. 40,* pp. 18-25. Nashville: Intellect Base International Consortium.